C000148062

EMBALADO EM PORTUGAL POR:

VINEYR...

ACEITE DE OLIVA
YBARRA

MAR. 00

1 LITRO

Para abrir, levantar uno d...
picos y cortar transversalm...
la punta. Servir manteniénd...
levantado sin aplastas...
laterales del paquete.

O&CO

HUILE D'OLIV...

vierg...

olive oil

olive oil

sauces, starters & mains

RYLAND
PETERS
& SMALL
LONDON NEW YORK

Designer Iona Hoyle
Senior Editor Clare Double
Picture Research Emily Westlake
Production Manager Patricia Harrington
Publishing Director Alison Starling

First published in the United Kingdom in 2007
by Ryland Peters & Small
20–21 Jockey's Fields
London WC1R 4BW
www.rylandpeters.com

10 9 8 7 6 5 4 3 2 1

Text © Maxine Clark, Clare Ferguson,
Clare Gordon-Smith, Laura Washburn 2007.
Design and photographs © Ryland Peters & Small 2007.
Text in this book has been previously published by
Ryland Peters & Small.

A CIP record for this book is available from the
British Library.
ISBN: 978-1-84597-392-6

Printed and bound in China

Notes
All spoon measurements are level unless
otherwise stated. Eggs are large unless
otherwise specified. Uncooked or partially
cooked eggs should not be served to the very
old, frail, young children, pregnant women or
those with compromised immune systems.

Ovens should be preheated to the specified
temperature. Recipes in this book were tested
with a regular oven. If using a fan-assisted
oven, decrease the temperature by 20°C (40°F),
or follow the manufacturer's instructions.

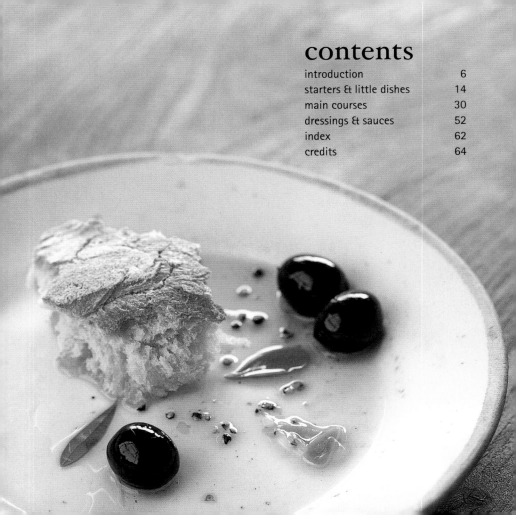

contents

a cultural icon

A bottle of really superb, estate-bottled, cold-pressed, extra virgin olive oil may cost more than the equivalent amount of champagne, since it takes about 5 kg of olives to make just 1 litre of this wonderful substance. But it is worth every penny. Olive oil is a nutritional marvel as well as a gastronomic joy. It keeps its distinctive, complex flavour and aroma and stays chemically intact because it contains health-giving nutrients such as tocopherol (vitamin E) to keep it stable. It is excellent for general cooking, and even for deep-frying, since it doesn't degrade during prolonged use at high temperatures.

For well over two millennia, olive trees, their fruit and their oil have been integral to the culture and eating habits of the Mediterranean – at the heart of Western culture. In fact olives and civilization have almost become synonymous. *Olea europaea*, the cultivated olive, has now spread to California, South Africa, Chile, Argentina, Australia, New Zealand and, surprisingly, China, but the myth of its 'Mediterranean' nature endures.

Today olive oil is one of the world's biggest health stories. We know that olive oil has revolutionary properties, mainly linked to its high levels of monounsaturated fatty acids, which could guard against arterial heart disease. In addition, because of its anti-oxidant properties, it can reduce free-radical damage in cells and therefore minimize the effects of ageing, and even protect against cancer.

making olive oil

It is reassuring to know that olive oil can be made from the pressed juices of the olive and nothing else, by law. In Italy and France, Spain and Portugal, many of the traditional terraced slopes and groves are now uneconomical to run, although prestigious regions in these countries, such as Liguria, Tuscany, Sardinia and Provence, still thrive. Spain and Greece continue to supply the market with large quantities of excellent extra virgin and virgin olive oils (some of which are blended to a degree of uniformity for the mass market). Increasingly, much production is being relocated to other Mediterranean sites such as Turkey and Tunisia, where the wage demands are lower and seasonal harvest workers more readily available, as are grants from EU sources.

The Harvest

By late autumn and early winter, the olives are green, succulent, and perfect for early-picked oil. Later, the fully ripe, purplish, dark-brown fruits will yield quite a different oil. Fully ripe olives produce the most oil and are therefore more profitable, but many believe the best oil is from green-ripe fruit because as they ripen, olives damage more easily and can fall and bruise, sustaining enzyme and oxidation damage that affects the taste.

Ideally, fruit to be pressed for oil should be picked by hand. This requires skill, patience and the absence of autumnal gales; olive picking is not only tricky but physically tiring. The fruit must be clean and free of twigs and leaves before crushing, and ideally reaches the pressing house, then is processed, within 36 hours. On small estates this is possible, but at a large plant there may be many olives from different sources waiting to be treated. They can become affected by the heat as they stand, which may compromise quality and flavour.

Extracting the Oil

Methods of extracting the oil vary from age-old and labour-intensive means to industrial centrifuging processes that traditionalists feel harm the taste and chemical structure of the oil. There are also intermediate methods including extraction using a centrifuge operating at gentler speeds, a rapid process popular with some producers. Finally there is filtering, tasting, blending, grading, bottling, labelling, and packaging.

grades and names

About a tenth of world production is top-class virgin oil, the purest form, of which there are four designated grades. The remainder is refined to remove flaws or impurities. Some of this refined olive oil is blended with virgin oils to create 'olive oil'; this tastes less good and is cheaper, but it is consistent and useful in its own right. The international olive oil trade grades oils on their amount of free acidity (which should be small) and on their smell and taste. They may also be chemically analysed to detect any unacceptable substances in the oil. Descriptions from the producer, such as 'first, cold-pressed', 'estate bottled' or 'unfiltered' can help you assess quality and style. Words such as 'lite' or 'light' are not official terms and so may be misleading.

Virgin olive oil

Any oil obtained solely from the olive by mechanical or other physical methods, under thermal conditions that do not cause any alteration of the oil. The only processes permitted are washing, extraction, decanting, centrifuging and filtering. The use of solvents is not permitted.

Extra virgin olive oil

Virgin oil of perfect aroma and flavour and of no more than 1 per cent free acidity. Many 'commercial' extra virgin olive oils are skilfully blended to a standard maintained from year to year, and to a price. They may come from different regions and countries. 'Single estate' products are often superb unblended oils, more expensive, and pronounced in flavour.

Virgin olive oil/fine olive oil

Virgin oil with a perfect aroma or flavour, but with free acidity of up to 2 per cent.

Ordinary/semi-fine virgin olive oil

Virgin oil of good but not perfect taste and aroma and with free acidity levels of up to 3.3 per cent.

Refined olive oil

Refined from virgin oils (generally lampantes) by processes which, by law, must not alter the oil's initial glyceride structure.

Olive oil/pure olive oil

Specific foodstuff terms used on a label to mean a blend of refined olive and virgin olive oil. Suitable for frying and general cooking where Mediterranean distinctiveness is not required.

what's on the label

First, cold-pressed
The very first pressing, with little or no heat applied. A superb product retaining its natural distinctiveness; often expensive.

Cold-pressed
Simply extracted without any heat above 28°C (82°F), but perhaps from the second pressing of the same olives. Still a good product, keeping many healthy qualities and flavour.

Estate-bottled/single estate
Top quality, premium-price oils, often from hand-picked olives and cold-pressed within hours of picking. Probably from one family estate or farm, it is grown, extracted and packaged on home ground. The Americas, Australia, New Zealand and even South Africa, as well as the great oil-producing areas of Europe, produce these oils.

Affiorato/flor de aceite/lágrima
Also known as 'flowers' or 'tears'. This is 'free run' oil – the olives will often have been roughly crushed, but not pressed: the oil merely runs off and is collected. This is rare and very desirable.

Date and year of pressing
Aim for oil as young as possible. Very new oil may be pungently bitter, but this softens within several months. No oil lasts well for more than a year.

Unfiltered
Means one less process and implies excellent oil and careful handling. Often murky, it is described as 'veiled', since 'cloudy' would imply a fault.

Single varietals/blends
The producer has used only one variety of olive, or a blend.

Designation of origin
Refers to oils from specific zones or regions that safeguard local traditions and olive types. In Spain it is called DO, in Greece PGI or PPO, in Italy DOC.

Organic/ecological production
Many small-scale oil producers and some co-operatives cultivate olives using organic methods approved by certified agencies.

Selecting olive oil
Choose a first cold-pressed or *affiorato* oil to trickle over food at the table. Cold-pressed, extra virgin oils (one peppery, one mellow) are useful for salads, pasta, soups and dressings. Keep cheaper extra virgin olive oil for general cooking and an ordinary virgin olive oil for mayonnaises and baking. 'Olive oil' (a blend of refined and virgin) can be used for deep-frying or bulk baking.

starters & little dishes

caponata

1 aubergine, about 300 g, cut into 1 cm cubes

1 tablespoon salt

4 tablespoons extra virgin olive oil

2 red onions, each cut in 8 wedges

4 garlic cloves, chopped

100 g dry-cured green olives

75 g dry-cured black olives

50 g capers in salt

2 teaspoons chopped fresh oregano, marjoram or thyme, plus extra sprigs, to serve (optional)

3 tomatoes, each cut in 8 wedges

2 baby courgettes, sliced crossways

2 tablespoons tomato purée

2 teaspoons sugar

150 ml chicken or vegetable stock or water

4 tablespoons chopped, fresh, flat leaf parsley, to serve

serves 6–8

This colourful dish is a classic Italian antipasto and comes from Sicily. It is also delicious with grilled fish or steak. Caponata may be served warm, cool or cold, but not chilled.

Sprinkle the aubergine with the salt, toss well and let stand for 10 minutes. Drain and pat dry with kitchen paper.

Put the oil in a large heavy-based saucepan and heat until very hot. Add the onions, garlic, olives and capers. Stir over high heat for 2–3 minutes, then add the aubergine and continue to cook, stirring, over medium heat for another 8 minutes. Using a slotted spoon, transfer the mixture to a plate and set aside.

Add the oregano, marjoram or thyme to the pan, then add the tomatoes, courgettes, tomato purée, sugar and stock or water. Stir gently and bring to the boil. Reduce the heat and simmer for 8 minutes. Return the aubergine mixture to the pan and simmer gently until the flavours have mingled. The vegetables should still be intact, not mushy. Dip the pan into a bowl of cold water to cool.

To serve, transfer to a bowl, sprinkle with parsley and top with the extra sprigs of oregano, marjoram or thyme, if using.

panzanella

3–4 thick slices crusty country bread, torn into pieces

2 red peppers, deseeded and cut into quarters

2 yellow peppers, deseeded and cut into quarters

500 g ripe, red, juicy tomatoes

3–4 garlic cloves, crushed to a purée

6–8 tablespoons extra virgin olive oil

1 tablespoon red wine vinegar

2 teaspoons balsamic vinegar

6 anchovy fillets, halved lengthways

6 caperberries or 2 tablespoons salted capers

a small bunch of basil

a few celery leaves (optional)

serves 4–6

A great summery or autumnal starter, this Tuscan dish has been interpreted worldwide. It needs superb, ripe, flavourful ingredients, so make it whenever you have wonderful sweet peppers, tomatoes and fresh, bouncy basil leaves.

Cut or pull the bread into 2 cm chunks or smaller and either leave plain or toast briefly under a preheated grill.

Cook the red and yellow peppers under a hot grill until the skins blister. Remove the skins and reserve the flesh. To prepare the tomatoes, cut a cross in the bottom, dip them into a saucepan of boiling water for about 30 seconds, then remove and pull off the skins. Put the tomatoes into a sieve set over a bowl to catch the juices. Cut or tear the tomatoes in half, then remove them and discard the seeds.

Cut the tomatoes into smaller pieces and put into the bowl of juice. Add the garlic, oil and two vinegars and stir to make a dressing.

Put the anchovies and caperberries into a bowl, cover with boiling water, let soak for 5 minutes, then drain, reserving the liquid.

Put the bread, tomatoes, peppers, caperberries, anchovies and half the basil into a bowl. Pour over the dressing and enough of the caperberry-anchovy soaking liquid to give a good flavour.

Toss gently and let stand for 10–20 minutes. Top with the reserved basil and celery leaves, if using, and serve.

bagna cauda

125 g unsalted butter, melted

6–8 garlic cloves, well crushed

90 ml extra virgin olive oil

100 g canned anchovy fillets, drained, chopped and mashed

your choice of:

red, yellow or orange peppers, deseeded and cut into 8 wedges

celery stalks

chicory • trevise

inner leaves from cos lettuce

spring onions • baby asparagus

cauliflower florets

broccoli florets, quartered lengthways

fennel bulbs, cut into wedges lengthways

sprigs of flat leaf parsley

serves 4–8

This intensely flavourful Italian dip is made with olive oil, although it may also be made with butter, particularly in the north. This version combines both methods, and speeds the process wonderfully. Amazingly, the result is mellow and smooth, not aggressively pungent at all. The crisp, sweet, mild vegetables offset the salty flavour of the sauce.

Put the butter and garlic into a non-stick frying pan and heat gently, until the butter has melted. Transfer to a blender and add the olive oil and anchovies. Purée for 2–3 minutes, then transfer to a serving bowl. The bowl of dip should be kept hot over a low candle flame.

Surround the hot dip with the cold, crisp vegetables and serve.

Note The traditional method is to put the butter and puréed garlic into a shallow terracotta dish and stir for 5–10 minutes over low to medium heat. Add the anchovy fillets and mash over the heat. Add the oil, reheat gently, then serve as above.

goats' cheeses marinated in olive oil

500 g small goats' cheeses, or large ones, sliced and quartered

600 ml virgin olive oil

75 g pitted black olives (optional)

4 garlic cloves

a selection of:

1 small red chilli, 2–3 sprigs of fresh thyme or rosemary, 2 bay leaves and 1 tablespoon peppercorns

lemon peel

sea salt

makes two 300 ml jars

Marinate your own goats' cheeses in olive oil – they can then be used grilled on toast, as a pasta sauce with snipped herbs, or served with a selection of crisp wafers.

Put the whole goats' cheeses in a clean Kilner jar or stoneware pot (see below). Pour in the olive oil, add salt, then push in the olives, if using. Blanch the garlic, your selection of herbs and spices and the lemon peel in boiling water for 1 minute, drain, then add to the jar.

Cover and leave to marinate in the refrigerator for 2 days before using within 1 week.

Sterilization of preserving jars Wash the jars in hot, soapy water and rinse in boiling water. Place in a large saucepan and then cover with hot water. With the lid on, bring the water to the boil and continue boiling for 15 minutes. Turn off the heat, then leave the jars in the hot water until just before they are to be filled. Invert the jars onto a clean kitchen towel to dry. Sterilize the lids for 5 minutes, by boiling, or according to the manufacturer's instructions.

olive oil and garlic bruschetta

4 large garlic cloves

6 tablespoons extra virgin olive oil

a good pinch chilli flakes

4 tablespoons chopped fresh parsley (optional)

for the bruschetta:

4 thick slices country bread, preferably sourdough

extra virgin olive oil, for drizzling

serves 4

This is pared-down simplicity and so easy to make. It beats the likes of doughballs and garlic bread hands down. The most important thing is not to overcook the garlic – it must on no account turn brown. This is great served instead of garlic bread with a selection of salads.

Slice the garlic lengthways into paper-thin slices. Heat a small pan, pour in the olive oil and stir in the garlic. Cook until the garlic starts to give off its aroma and is golden but not brown (or it will taste bitter). Remove from the heat, then mix in the chilli flakes and parsley, if using. Cover to keep warm.

To make the bruschetta, grill, toast or pan-grill the bread on both sides until lightly charred or toasted, then drizzle with olive oil. Spoon or brush over the garlicky chilli oil and eat immediately.

moroccan-style marinated black olives

750 g black olives in brine

2 tablespoons fennel or cumin seeds, crushed

1 tablespoon green cardamom pods, crushed

1 tablespoon small, hot, dried red chillies

2 tablespoons allspice berries, crushed

850 ml extra virgin olive oil

20 cm strip of orange zest, bruised

12 fresh bay leaves, washed, dried and bruised

makes one 1.5 litre jar or three 500 ml jars

Black olives which have already been cured will mellow even more if you crack them a little or prick them with a fork, then marinate in spices and fine olive oil. Experiment until you find a flavour you like – your own customized blend. This is an aromatic Moroccan-inspired version; you could even use Moroccan olive oil for an authentic result.

Rinse the olives in cold water, drain, then pat dry with kitchen paper. Put them on a clean dry surface and crush them slightly with a meat hammer or rolling pin, or prick with a fork, to open the flesh a little.

Put the fennel seeds, cardamom, chillies and allspice in a dry frying pan and toast over a moderate heat for a few minutes until aromatic.

Put the olive oil in a saucepan and heat to 180°C (350°F) – a cube of bread should turn golden-brown in 40–50 seconds. Let cool a little. Using a sterilized spoon, pack the zest, bay leaves, olives and spices into a clean jar (see below) in layers. Cover with the hot olive oil. Let cool, uncovered. When cold, seal and store in a cool, dark place.

Leave for at least 1 week before tasting. These olives keep well and improve for some months.

Note See page 20 for information on sterilizing preserving jars.

focaccia with olives

7 g sachet easy-blend dried yeast

250 g plain white flour, plus
4 tablespoons for shaping

½ teaspoon sea salt flakes

2 tablespoons extra virgin olive
oil, preferably Italian

topping:

finely shredded zest of 1 orange

grated zest and freshly squeezed
juice of 1 orange

4 tablespoons extra virgin olive oil

2 garlic cloves, crushed

2 tablespoons fresh rosemary
leaves, coarsely chopped

½ teaspoon coarsely crushed
black pepper

1 teaspoon sea salt flakes
or crystals

150 g dry-cured black olives

serves 4

This focaccia dough is a quick food processor version with olive oil in the topping and the dough. This is practical and delicious, since there is no need to rub the flour in. You could use lemon instead of orange, oregano rather than rosemary, or other toppings such as anchovy-stuffed green olives.

Put the yeast, flour and sea salt into a food processor fitted with a plastic blade. Pulse briefly to sift the ingredients. Mix the oil and 180 ml warm water and, with the machine running, pour it in all at once through the feed tube. Process, in short bursts, for 15 seconds until a soft mass forms (not a ball). It will be sticky and soft.

Scoop out the dough. Add the extra 4 tablespoons flour as you knead and thump the dough for 2 minutes. Put the ball of dough into an oiled bowl and enclose the bowl in a large plastic bag. Leave in a warm place until the dough has doubled in size, about 50 minutes.

Pat and stretch the dough into a rectangle about 32 x 22 cm. Transfer to an oiled oven tray. Prod the dough all over with your fingertips to form dimples to take the topping.

Mix the orange zests and juice, oil, garlic, rosemary, pepper and half the salt, and pour over the dough. Scatter with the olives, pushing well into the dimples. Set aside for 30 minutes to rest the dough.

Bake in a preheated oven at 200°C (400°F) Gas 6 for 25–30 minutes or until crusty and aromatic. Sprinkle with the remaining salt. Cut into generous squares, then serve hot or warm.

rosemary, raisin and olive oil bread

1 tablespoon dried active yeast

3 tablespoons caster sugar

400 g plain white flour, warmed (but not hot)

2 large sprigs fresh rosemary, washed and dried

6 tablespoons extra virgin olive oil

150 g raisins, sultanas or dried muscatel grapes

makes 6 rolls

These rosemary-flavoured buns were traditionally eaten in Italy on Maundy Thursday. The olive oil is essential for a good flavour, so use the best. Raisins are traditional, but chopped ready-to-eat figs make a delicious alternative.

Dissolve the yeast and 1 teaspoon of the sugar in 250 ml warm water and leave to stand for 10 minutes until frothy.

Sift the flour into a bowl, add the remaining sugar, then make a well in the centre and add the yeast liquid. Mix until it comes together, then knead on a lightly floured work surface for 10 minutes until elastic. Put the dough in a clean bowl, cover with clingfilm and leave to rise in a warm place for about 1½ hours.

Meanwhile, strip off the rosemary leaves and lightly bruise them with the end of a rolling pin. Heat them with 4 tablespoons of the olive oil in a small pan. Remove from the heat and cool. Strain when cold.

Uncover the dough and knock it back. Tip out onto the work surface and knead in the cooled olive oil and rosemary with the raisins. Pull the dough into 6, shape into balls, then put on a floured baking sheet and flatten slightly. Using a very sharp knife, make two cuts along the top of each roll, then two across, like a grid. Cover and leave in a warm place for 30–40 minutes until doubled in size.

Uncover and brush with the remaining olive oil. Bake in a preheated oven at 180°C (350°F) Gas 4 for 30 minutes until risen and brown, and the rolls sound hollow when tapped on the bottom.

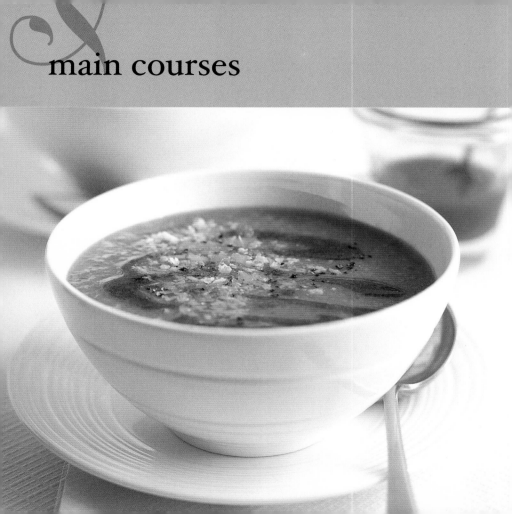

main courses

creamy tomato and bread soup with basil oil

1.5 litres vegetable, chicken or meat stock

4 tablespoons olive oil

1 onion, chopped

1.25 kg very ripe, soft tomatoes, coarsely chopped

300 g stale white bread, thinly sliced, crusts removed (or breadcrumbs)

3 garlic cloves, crushed

125 g freshly grated Parmesan cheese, plus extra to serve

sea salt and freshly ground black pepper

basil oil:

6 tablespoons freshly chopped basil

150 ml extra virgin olive oil

serves 6

For this comforting soup you need great tomatoes, good bread and wonderful, green olive oil. The leftover bread thickens this rich tomato soup, which is in turn enriched with Parmesan. In Tuscany, where this dish comes from, you would be given olive oil at the table to pour over the soup yourself, but here basil oil is used instead.

Heat the stock slowly in a large saucepan. Meanwhile, heat the oil in a second large saucepan, add the onion and tomatoes and fry over gentle heat for about 10 minutes until soft. Push the mixture through a food mill, mouli or sieve, and stir into the hot broth. Add the bread and garlic.

Cover and simmer gently for about 45 minutes until thick and creamy, whisking from time to time to break up the bread. Take care, because this soup can catch on the bottom.

Meanwhile, to make the basil oil, put the basil and olive oil in a blender and blend until completely smooth – if not, pour through a fine strainer.

To finish, stir the Parmesan into the soup, then add salt and pepper to taste. Ladle into bowls and trickle 2 tablespoons basil oil over each serving. Serve hot, warm or cold (not chilled), with more Parmesan.

creamy wheat and bean soup with rosemary

300 g dried borlotti beans

100 g dried chickpeas

a pinch of bicarbonate of soda

6 tablespoons extra virgin olive oil, plus extra to drizzle

2 garlic cloves, finely chopped

2 tablespoons chopped fresh rosemary

1 tablespoon tomato purée diluted with 100 ml warm water

250 g Italian farro or whole spelt grains

sea salt and freshly ground black pepper

serves 6

Italian farro is a very ancient grain, cultivated by the Romans until wheat overtook it in popularity. It is a close relation of the grain spelt, which makes a good alternative. Cooked with beans, it makes a creamy, nutty soup, delicious served with thick slices of country bread.

Soak the beans and the chickpeas overnight in abundant cold water. Drain, then cook with a pinch of bicarbonate of soda in a large pan of boiling water for 45 minutes to 1 hour until tender. Drain, reserving 2 litres of the cooking water. Mash the beans a little to start them disintegrating, then set aside.

Heat the oil in a medium saucepan and add the garlic and rosemary. Cook for 1 minute until the garlic turns light golden and the rosemary releases its fragrance. Add the diluted tomato purée, then pour in the reserved cooking water. Bring to the boil, then stir in the farro. Season with salt and pepper and simmer gently for 1 hour or until the farro is al dente.

Stir in the lightly mashed bean mixture. Taste and adjust the seasoning, being generous with the pepper. Reheat, adding extra water if the soup is too thick. Serve in large bowls with extra virgin olive oil to drizzle over the top.

mozzarella, tomato and rocket salad

3 x 150 g buffalo
mozzarella cheeses

4 large, juicy, ripe red tomatoes

4 large handfuls of fresh wild
rocket, about 350 g

6–8 tablespoons first-pressed
extra virgin olive oil

sea salt and freshly ground
black pepper

serves 4

The famous Italian caprese salad normally includes basil.
In this variation, rocket adds a peppery bite. Find milky, soft
buffalo mozzarella, which has a better flavour than the
cows' milk version. Add ripe, flavourful tomatoes and an
exceptional extra virgin olive oil, and this dish becomes
sublime. Eat it immediately, and never refrigerate this salad.

Drain the mozzarellas. Slice thickly or pull them apart into big rough
chunks, showing the grainy strands. Arrange down one side of a
large serving platter.

Slice the tomatoes thickly and arrange them in a second line down
the middle of the plate. If the slices are very large, halve them. Add
the wild rocket leaves down the other side of the platter.

Sprinkle with salt and pepper, then just before serving trickle the
olive oil over the top. Make sure you have some crusty bread
(slightly char-grilled tastes good) to mop up the juices.

salad of wild greens

2 handfuls peppery leaves, such as rocket or watercress

2 handfuls bitter leaves, such as endive, batavia or frisée

2 handfuls crisp green lettuce, such as Little Gem, torn

1 small head chicory, separated into leaves

1 small head radicchio, separated into leaves

leaves from 1 small bunch of flat leaf parsley, dill or mint (optional)

1 small red onion

dressing:

2 garlic cloves, crushed

½ teaspoon sea salt flakes

1–1½ tablespoons freshly squeezed lemon juice

4–6 tablespoons extra virgin olive oil, preferably Greek or Italian

serves 4

In Greece and Italy wonderful selections of baby green leaves and herbs are gathered from gardens and fields in spring and summer, from wild samphire to dandelion greens, rocket, wild mustard, curly endive, purslane, radish and beetroot leaves. The ingredients here are guidelines for you to assemble your own wild salad.

To make the dressing, put the garlic, salt and half the lemon juice in a small bowl and mix with a hand-held blender. Drizzle in the oil and blend until a rich emulsion forms. Taste, then add enough lemon juice to give bite.

Alternatively, use a mortar and pestle to pound the garlic and salt to a sticky paste. Drizzle in the oil, continuing to pound and stir until a rich emulsion forms. Add lemon juice to taste.

Wash the leaves and herbs, if using. Finely slice the onion into rings. Put the leaves, herbs and onion rings in a large bowl. Cover with a plastic bag, seal and chill until ready to serve, so the leaves stay crisp and fresh.

Just before serving, trickle the dressing over the leaves and toss thoroughly with your hands or 2 wooden spoons.

spanish roasted vegetable salad

2 red peppers

2 yellow peppers

½ butternut squash or 500 g pumpkin, unpeeled

2 red onions, unpeeled

2 Spanish onions, unpeeled

125 ml extra virgin olive oil, preferably Spanish

4 medium-sized, vine-ripened tomatoes

sea salt and freshly ground black pepper

serves 4–6

A classic Spanish dish full of sweet summer bounty. It can be served hot, warm or cool, and is especially good accompanied by country bread and a lively Spanish wine such as Rioja or Rosado.

Cut the peppers in half lengthways, slicing through the stems. Leave these intact but discard the pith and seeds.

Slice the squash or pumpkin into 2.5 cm discs or chunks.

Cut all the onions crossways into halves, leaving the roots and tops intact. Leave the skins on too – they give extra colour and flavour and protect the shape.

Put the peppers, squash or pumpkin and onions, cut sides up, in a large, lightly oiled roasting tin. Drizzle half the oil over the vegetables and sprinkle with sea salt and pepper.

Roast near the top of a preheated oven at 240°C (475°F) Gas 9 for 30 minutes, until the vegetables are frizzled, wrinkled and soft. Add the tomatoes for the last 10 minutes of cooking time.

Drizzle the remaining oil over the top and serve hot, warm or cool. Eat the salad with your fingers, discarding the skins, roots and stems along the way. This is superb with bread to scoop up the sweet, oily, sticky juices from the hot tin.

stewed fennel with olive oil, lemon and chilli

4 medium heads of fennel

200 ml extra virgin olive oil

finely grated zest and
freshly squeezed juice of 1 large
unwaxed lemon

1 anchovy in oil or salt, rinsed and
finely chopped

½ teaspoon chilli flakes

a little white wine vinegar
(optional)

sea salt and freshly ground
black pepper

serves 4–6

In this dish, the fennel absorbs all the flavours of the olive oil, lemon juice and chilli, and the anchovy adds a salty touch. Braising the fennel slowly makes it meltingly soft and tender. This is delicious with pork and robust fish like swordfish, and can be made in advance; it only improves with keeping and is better the next day.

Trim the stalks and fronds from the fennel. Discard the stalks, but keep the green fronds. Halve the fennel bulbs. Cut out the hard core, then cut each half into 2 wedges. Arrange the fennel wedges in a flameproof baking dish.

Put the olive oil, lemon zest and juice, anchovy, chilli flakes, vinegar, if using, salt and pepper in a bowl and whisk well. Pour over the fennel. Bring the dish to the boil on top of the stove. Cover with kitchen foil and bake in a preheated oven at 160°C (325°F) Gas 3 for 1 hour or until very soft and tender.

Remove from the oven and remove the foil. Taste the liquid and add a dash of vinegar to sharpen it if necessary. Serve warm or cold, sprinkled with the reserved fennel fronds.

ratatouille

1 kg aubergines, cut into pieces

extra virgin olive oil (see method)

2 medium onions, coarsely chopped

2 red peppers, 2 yellow peppers, and 1 green pepper, halved, deseeded and cut into pieces

6 small courgettes, about 750 g, halved lengthways and sliced

4 garlic cloves, crushed

6 medium tomatoes, halved, deseeded and chopped

a small bunch of basil, coarsely chopped

coarse sea salt

to serve:

a few basil leaves, finely sliced

1 garlic clove, crushed

serves 4–6

To make this ratatouille, you add each vegetable separately, in the order that best suits its cooking requirements. Each vegetable 'layer' must be seasoned individually. Cut the vegetable pieces medium-large, about 3–4 cm, to keep the flavours distinct from each other. Serve with crusty bread.

Put the aubergine pieces and 3 tablespoons water in a microwave-proof bowl. Microwave on HIGH for 6 minutes, drain and set aside.

Heat 3 tablespoons oil in a large casserole with a lid. Add the onions and cook until soft, 3–5 minutes. Salt lightly.

Add all the peppers and cook for 5–8 minutes more, stirring often. Turn up the heat to keep the sizzling sound going, but take care not to let it burn. Salt lightly.

Add 1 more tablespoon oil and the courgettes. Mix well and cook for about 5 minutes more, stirring occasionally. Salt lightly.

Add 2 more tablespoons oil and the drained aubergines. Cook, stirring often, for 5 minutes more. Salt lightly.

Add the garlic and cook for 1 minute. Add the tomatoes and basil plus 1 more tablespoon oil if necessary, and stir well. Salt lightly. Cook for 5 minutes, then cover, lower the heat and simmer gently for 30 minutes, checking occasionally.

Remove from the heat. Serve at room temperature, stirring in extra basil and garlic just before serving.

roast peppers stuffed with pasta and tomatoes

4 medium yellow or red peppers

50 g very fine spaghetti

6 tablespoons extra virgin olive oil

12 ripe cherry tomatoes, quartered

2 garlic cloves, finely chopped

3 tablespoons chopped fresh basil

50 g pine nuts, coarsely chopped

75 g freshly grated pecorino cheese

½ teaspoon dried chilli flakes (optional)

sea salt and freshly ground black pepper

serves 4

These peppers are a vegetable and pasta course in one. They should be luscious and soft, with a wrinkled, browned exterior. The garlicky cherry tomatoes keep the pasta moist, and the chilli and pecorino give a hint of sharpness. This is a good accompaniment for fish.

Slice the tops off the peppers and reserve. Scrape out and discard all the seeds and white pith. Set the peppers upright in a lightly oiled dish small enough to fit them snugly. If they don't stand upright, shave a little piece off the base, but not right through.

Cook the pasta in plenty of boiling salted water until just al dente, about 8 minutes or according to the package instructions. Drain well and toss with 2 tablespoons of the olive oil.

Put the tomatoes in a bowl with another 2 tablespoons of oil, the garlic, basil, pine nuts, pecorino and chilli flakes, if using, and mix well. Add the pasta to the peppers, filling them by two-thirds, then spoon in the tomato mixture. Put the pepper lids on top and brush liberally all over with the remaining olive oil.

Bake in a preheated oven at 220°C (425°F) Gas 7 for 25–30 minutes or until the peppers start to wrinkle and blister. Serve hot or at room temperature.

chicken with tomato, garlic and olives

2 tablespoons extra virgin olive oil

1 free-range chicken, about 2 kg, cut into 6–8 pieces

8 garlic cloves, finely chopped

400 g canned chopped tomatoes

a pinch of sugar

50 g black olives, preferably niçoise, pitted and coarsely chopped

a bunch of fresh basil, torn

coarse sea salt and freshly ground black pepper

serves 4–6

This hearty chicken dish is found all over France, but the south-eastern version here has particularly assertive flavours. It goes well with rice or fresh pasta, such as the saffron tagliatelle pictured here.

Heat 1 tablespoon of the oil in a large sauté pan. Add the chicken pieces and brown on all sides. Transfer the chicken to a plate, salt generously and set aside. Add the remaining oil and garlic and cook for 1 minute; do not let it burn. Add the tomatoes and sugar. Stir well and return the chicken pieces to the pan. Cover and simmer gently until the chicken is cooked, 25–30 minutes.

Transfer the chicken pieces to a serving dish, then raise the heat and cook the sauce to thicken slightly, about 10 minutes. Add salt and pepper to taste, then stir in the olives. Pour the sauce over the chicken pieces, sprinkle with the basil and serve immediately.

greek chicken stifado

1 free-range chicken, about
1.5 kg, whole or quartered, or
4 breast or leg portions

2 tablespoons extra virgin olive oil

10 whole cloves

20 pearl onions or
10 shallots, halved

8 canned artichokes, drained

4 garlic cloves, chopped

2 tablespoons white wine vinegar
or lemon juice

6 tablespoons rich tomato purée
(double strength)

450 g canned chopped tomatoes

24 black olives, such as Kalamata

a large bunch fresh or dried
rosemary, oregano, thyme
or a mixture

freshly ground black pepper

serves 4

In Greece *stifado* can refer to a number of things, but essentially it is a thickened stew with tomato, garlic and olive oil – perfect for winter. Sometimes made with beef or rabbit, guinea fowl or even quail, it is a handsome dish, easy to prepare, and fragrant with herbs. Serve from the dish, accompanied by torn country bread, noodles or rice.

Pat the chicken dry with kitchen paper. Heat the olive oil in a large flameproof casserole, add the chicken and sauté for 8–10 minutes, turning it with tongs from time to time.

Push the cloves into some of the onions and add them all to the pan. Add the artichokes, garlic, vinegar, tomato purée, tomatoes, olives and freshly ground black pepper. Tuck in the herb sprigs around the edges.

Bring to the boil and reduce the heat to low. Cover and simmer for 30 minutes for chicken pieces, or about 60 minutes if using a whole bird, or until the chicken seems tender and the sauce has reduced and thickened.

provençal beef daube with lemon and parsley

1 kg beef topside or blade steak, cut 3 cm thick

2 tablespoons extra virgin olive oil

10 garlic cloves, sliced

250 g cubed unsmoked bacon

2 red onions, quartered

4 medium carrots, left whole

6 plum tomatoes, cut into wedges

1 unwaxed lemon and grated zest

1 fresh bouquet garni of thyme, bay, parsley and oregano

75 g prunes

250 ml rich red wine

200 ml boiling beef stock

a bunch of flat leaf parsley, freshly chopped

2 tablespoons fresh brioche or breadcrumbs (optional)

sea salt and freshly ground black pepper

serves 4

This is a simplified version of a classic stew, left bubbling for hours, enriched with bacon and fragrant with red wine. It's straightforward, so there's time to make the aromatic lemon, parsley and garlic topping, gremolata (which is not Provençal, but Italian). The lemon adds extra vibrancy to the dish. Like most stews, this will improve over several days.

Beat the beef all over with a meat hammer or rolling pin, then cut it into 5 cm square chunks. Heat the oil in a large flameproof casserole, add the beef, in batches if necessary, and sauté for 4 minutes on each side. Remove with a slotted spoon and set aside.

Add 2 of the garlic cloves to the pan, then add the bacon, onions and carrots. Stir and sauté until the bacon is golden and the fat has run. Add the tomatoes, half the lemon zest, the bouquet garni, prunes, wine and stock. Replace the browned beef, pushing the pieces well down under the liquid.

Remove the white pith from the lemon. Cut the flesh into tiny cubes and add to the pan, to give flavour and tenderness to the meat.

Reduce the heat to a gentle simmer. Cover with a lid and cook, undisturbed, for 1½ hours, then test for doneness. (If preferred, cook in a low oven at 150°C (300°F) Gas 2 for 2½ hours or until tender.)

To make the gremolata, chop the remaining garlic and mix with the remaining lemon zest, the parsley and breadcrumbs, if using. Serve the daube with its sauce and the gremolata sprinkled on top.

dressings & sauces

hoummus

200 g dried chickpeas (if possible, without skins), or 400 g cooked

freshly squeezed juice of 1 lemon

2 garlic cloves, crushed

¼ teaspoon salt

2 tablespoons tahini paste (optional)

125 ml first-pressing extra virgin olive oil

freshly ground black pepper

to serve:

hot paprika

extra virgin olive oil

makes 400 ml

Fresh, lemony hoummus makes a delicious snack – add the sesame richness of tahini to give a more intense effect. Excellent olive oil utterly defines the flavour: use a beauty. For 10-minute hoummus, use canned chickpeas.

If using dried chickpeas, put them in a bowl and cover with boiling water for 3 hours (or in cold water for 8 hours). Drain. Put in a large saucepan, cover with boiling water, bring to the boil, part-cover and simmer for 1½–2½ hours or until the chickpeas are easily crushable and tender. Drain.

Put the chickpeas in a food processor with the lemon juice, garlic, salt, pepper and the tahini paste, if using. Blend briefly to a mousse. With the machine running, drizzle the oil through the feed tube to form a creamy purée. Season to taste.

Serve cool or chilled, sprinkled with a little hot red paprika and with the traditional trickle of extra virgin olive oil. Accompany with crisp lettuce leaves and heated, torn or cut flatbreads as well as other crisp raw vegetables.

classic vinaigrette

75 ml white or red wine vinegar

375 ml extra virgin olive oil

sea salt and freshly ground
white pepper

makes 450 ml

The simplest olive oil dressing is a drizzle of best-quality extra virgin oil, followed by a few drops of aged balsamic vinegar. This classic vinaigrette is an emulsion of oil and vinegar with, if you wish, seasonings such as mustard.

Put all the ingredients in a bowl, vinaigrette flask or screw-top jar. Whisk, beat or shake to form a temporary emulsion. Store in a cool, dark place, since rancidity can occur in bright sunlight and heat. Use within a week – and shake again to mix before use.

To make a smaller amount – enough for one salad – use 1 part vinegar to 5 parts oil, plus seasoning to taste. If preferred, pour the ingredients into the base of the salad bowl and beat them with a fork. Put the salad on top and leave undisturbed (no longer than about 30 minutes), then toss just before serving.

mustard vinaigrette

Add 1 tablespoon hot mustard powder or mixed mustard such as Dijon. This will create a stable emulsion and add bite.

lemon and anchovy vinaigrette

Use lemon juice instead of vinegar. Pound 6 canned anchovy fillets with the pepper and some of the lemon juice. Add about 2 tablespoons tiny pickled capers and mix with the oil.

simple mayonnaise

2 egg yolks, at room temperature

2 teaspoons Dijon mustard

¼ teaspoon salt

2 teaspoons freshly squeezed lemon juice or white wine vinegar

200 ml extra virgin olive oil

175 ml light oil, such as grapeseed, safflower or sunflower oil

makes 400 ml

Egg yolks, with a little acidity and seasoning, at the right temperature and degree of agitation, have the miraculous ability to absorb huge volumes of oil to form a rich, thick emulsion and this classic sauce. Many find olive oil alone too intense a taste, so here it is blended with a lighter oil.

Put the egg yolks into a medium bowl with high, straight sides and a curved base. Stir in the mustard, salt and half the lemon juice and beat until smooth.

Mix the oils in a small jug then, with the oil jug in one hand and an electric, hand-held whisk in the other, gradually drizzle the oil into the egg yolks, whisking continuously to form a stiff, glossy emulsion. When all the oil has been added, taste, then whisk or beat in the remaining lemon juice. Taste and adjust the seasoning. Cover the surface with clingfilm until ready to use. Best used immediately, mayonnaise may also be refrigerated for up to 3 days.

aioli

Pound the salt with 4 garlic cloves to form a sticky paste, beat in the eggs, then proceed as in the main recipe.

tarragon mayonnaise

Use tarragon vinegar and add 2 teaspoons blanched, chopped tarragon leaves to the finished mayonnaise. This is superb with chicken, poached fish and eggs.

classic pesto

100 g pine nuts

125 ml extra virgin olive oil

6 garlic cloves, chopped

1 teaspoon coarse sea salt
or rock salt

25 g fresh basil leaves, torn

50 g freshly grated Parmesan
cheese

50 g freshly grated pecorino
cheese

makes about 375 g

Italy calls it pesto, France calls it pistou – but this family of sauces is always a mixture of fresh herbs blended to a paste with garlic, salt and good olive oil. Basil is traditional, but other good sauces can be made with parsley or rocket, while coriander gives it a Middle Eastern or Asian flavour. Most contain cheeses and some include nuts, usually pine nuts.

Put the pine nuts in a small frying pan, add 1 teaspoon of the olive oil and stir-fry quickly until golden. Remove and let cool.

Put the pine nuts, garlic, salt and basil in a food processor and work to a paste. Alternatively, use a mortar and pestle. Still working, add half the cheese, then gradually pour in half the olive oil. Add the remaining cheese and oil all at once and work or blend one last time. The paste should be a vivid green.

coriander pesto

Use half parsley and half coriander instead of the basil. Use almonds in place of pine nuts and use all Parmesan, not a mixture.

rocket pesto

Replace half the basil with rocket; this gives a bitter edge that tastes curiously good.

black olive paste

500 g dry-cured black olives

25 g capers, rinsed,
about 2 tablespoons

8 canned anchovy fillets,
rinsed and chopped

½ teaspoon freshly ground
black pepper

1 teaspoon dried oregano,
marjoram or thyme

1 small, hot chilli, finely
chopped, or 1 garlic clove,
chopped (optional)

100 ml extra virgin olive oil

to serve:

75–100 g *carta da musica*,
grissini (Italian breadsticks) or
other flatbreads

1–2 tablespoons extra virgin
olive oil

serves 4–6

This paste is pungently delicious and makes a perfect starter. It is traditionally served with a Sardinian flatbread, *carta da musica*, which is often dried into crisp, brittle round sheets, but breadsticks or another flatbread make good substitutes.

If you are serving the paste with flatbreads, brush one side with 1–2 tablespoons of olive oil. Transfer to a preheated oven and cook at 200°C (400°F) Gas 6 for 8–10 minutes, then turn off the oven and leave the door slightly ajar.

To make the paste, remove and discard the pits from the olives. Put the olives into a food processor, then add the capers, anchovies, pepper, dried herb and chilli or garlic, if using.

Chop the mixture in several short, pulsing bursts. With the machine running, slowly pour in the oil through the feed tube, until the mixture forms a rich, coarse purée. Don't over-process: some contrast in texture is important.

Serve the olive paste with the hot flatbreads. The paste may be stored in the refrigerator for up to 2 weeks.

index

credits

Photography Credits

Key: a=above, b=below, r=right, l=left.

Peter Cassidy: Endpapers, page 4, 5, 8bl, 13, 14, 17, 18, 25, 26, 29, 33, 34, 37, 38, 45, 55, 56, 61, 62

Martin Brigdale: Pages 6–7, 8al, 8ar, 30, 41, 42, 46, 49, 50

Nicki Dowey: Pages 1, 59

William Lingwood: Pages 52, 64

Chris Tubbs: Pages 8br, 10

Gus Filgate: Page 22

James Merrell: Page 21

Diana Miller: Page 3

Recipe Credits

Introduction text and recipes by
Clare Ferguson except for the following:

Maxine Clark: Pages 23, 28, 31, 32, 40, 44

Laura Washburn: Pages 43, 47

Clare Gordon-Smith: Page 20

ACEITE DE OLIVA
VIRGEN EXTRA
GRAN PREMIO EN LA
Exposicion Hispano-Francesa
DE
ZARAGOZA
PRIMERA CASA EXPORTADORA
DE ESPAÑA
CARBONELL y Cia

SANT'E FORTI
PALERMO
A GOCCE

OLIVA
VIRGEN EXTRA

CARBONELL